THE BRINK

First Edition

02 01 00   3 2 1

Copyright © 2000 by Peter Sears

Published by

Gibbs Smith, Publisher

P.O. Box 667

Layton, UT 84041

Orders: (1-800) 748-5439

Visit our Web site at *www.gibbs-smith.com*

Cover designed by Gary Young

Text designed by Leesha Jones

Text edited by Gail Yngve

Book printed and bound in the United States of America

The cover art, *Freefall,* by Helen Frankenthaler, is printed and published by Tyler
Graphics Ltd. © copyright Helen Frankenthaler/Tyler Graphics Ltd., 1992.
Photo: Steve Sloman, New York.

LIBRARY OF CONGRESS CATALOGING-IN-PUBLICATION DATA

Sears, Peter
        The brink / Peter Sears.— 1st ed.
            p. cm
        ISBN 0-87905-924-9
            I. Title.

PS3569.E19 B75 2000

813'.54—dc21   99-089859

THE BRINK

◆

PETER SEARS

SALT LAKE CITY

Some of these poems have appeared in the following magazines in their original form or since revised.

Antioch Review: "Slip Away"

The Atlantic: "Oil Spill"

Black Warrior Review: "Inmates Work at the Chicken Factory"

Chowder Review: "Ash"

Cimarron Review: "Dumbo Diner"

Continental Drift: "Halloween of the Sudden Hand"

Drive, They Said: Milkweed Editions:
"When the Big Blue Light Comes a Whirling Up Behind"

Fiddlehead: "Snake Mouth"

Hanging Loose: "Wax Stuns Precision Grinding,
Sweeps to City Softball Title"

Hubbub: "Do Not Let Them Take Me Away If Naked";
"How They're Dancing Is How They Eat"

Left Bank: "Down a Well"

New Letters: "The Man Who Lives on Air"

Northwest Literary Forum: "Coming Home"

Let Us Drink to the River: An Anthology of River Poems:
"Night Fishing"

Mademoiselle: "After Tedious Arguing"

Many Mountains Moving: "Some of the Dead Go to the City"

Mother Jones: "Big Shot Graces the Old Bar & Grill"

Northwest Review: "The Brink"; "The Clearing";
"What Scared Me As a Boy Was Not My Sex"

Orion: "Snow at Night"

Outsiders: Poems About Rebels, Exiles, and Renegades:
Milkweed Editions: "The One Polar Bear"

Poet & Critic: "Standing Water"

Portlandia Review of Books: "Information Blackout"

Prescott Street Reader: "Bad Day"

Seattle Review: "I Won't Need Legs There"

Willow Springs: "Birds That Beat the Sky to Bits";
"I Might Break; I Might Disappear"; "Men and Fat";
"Shoveling Snow While It's Still Snowing";
"Glint"; "Full Heat That Flutters"

Xanadu: "A Man on a Bicycle"; "Victim"

Zyzzyva: "Traffic Jam on the Ross Island Bridge"

◆

To my wife, Anita

THE BRINK

CONTENTS

I

OLD, VERY OLD: A SERIES OF POEMS IN AN OLD VOICE

5 ✦ Snow at Night

6 ✦ Birds That Beat the Sky to Bits

7 ✦ Standing Water

8 ✦ I Might Break, I Might Disappear

9 ✦ Slip Away

10 ✦ Men and Fat

11 ✦ Bad Day

12 ✦ Glint

13 ✦ Blue Blue Hair

14 ✦ I Won't Need Legs There

15 ✦ Do Not Let Them Take Me Away If Naked

16 ✦ Shoveling Snow While It Is Still Snowing

17 ✦ Full Heat That Flutters

18 ✦ How They're Dancing Is How They Eat

II

NIGHT FISHING

23 ✦ The One Polar Bear

24 ✦ Down a Well

25 ✦ The Fox

26 ✦ Wax Stuns Precision Grinding, Sweeps to City Softball Title

28 ✦ Halloween of the Sudden Hand

29 ✦ Snake Mouth

30 ✦ Coming Home

32 ♦ The Man Who Can't Wait for Burglars

33 ♦ Odysseus Turns Pro

34 ♦ When the Dirt Won't Stay Down

35 ♦ When the Big Blue Light Comes a Whirling Up Behind

36 ♦ A Man on a Bicycle

37 ♦ Traffic Jam on the Ross Island Bridge

38 ♦ The One Time I Got Back to My Birth

39 ♦ After Tedious Arguing

40 ♦ Night Fishing

41 ♦ Some of the Dead Go to the City

III

MALENESS AND VIOLENCE

47 ♦ The Brink

48 ♦ The Clearing

49 ♦ What Scared Me As a Boy Was Not My Sex

50 ♦ Victim

52 ♦ Oil Spill

53 ♦ Inmates Work at the Chicken Factory

54 ♦ Dumbo Diner

56 ♦ Ash

58 ♦ The Man Who Lives on Air

59 ♦ Junk Is My Life

60 ♦ Big Shot Graces the Old Bar & Grill

62 ♦ The Distance

63 ♦ Pulling It Out

64 ♦ Information Blackout

66 ♦ They Came Here to Die

67 ♦ Moriches Bay

◆

The trouble with me is that whether I get love or not
I suffer from it.

—C. K. WILLIAMS, *ON THE ROOF*

I

OLD, VERY OLD
A SERIES OF POEMS IN AN OLD VOICE

◆

SNOW AT NIGHT

I am so far away
that from there I can hear myself talking to someone
and an echo like when you turn away from a river
and you can't tell
if it's the river right then
or a sound of the river echoing through you.

I want to go there and watch in the eddies near the shore
The caught sticks turning, then popping back,
then turning again,
as if they would break in two to shake free.

I'm like the snow at night in the field.
Most of the time you can't see it, then it glistens.

BIRDS THAT BEAT THE SKY TO BITS

The old biddy was a fool, but when she went,
she left a hole big enough to fall in.
The old coot next door isn't much better,
about as much fun as old bread. Always out
clipping his bushes, and when I went by,
he nodded, tipped his hat. When he looks up now,
into the mirror, he doesn't know sometimes
he is there. That's the stroke. One minute
you're someone, the next you're not.

He doesn't come out anymore. If he wanted to,
and stand by his bushes, I would stand
with him. If he got to feeling pretty good,
I would take him to where the birds
settle in the flyway, and be there
for the first time they all lift.
Oh my, the screeching and flapping
as if they will beat the sky to bits!
I'll say "migration." Maybe he will too.
I'll say "migration my gracious!" It's fun.
He may get a laugh out of that. We can laugh,
you know, even when we are pretty shot.

STANDING WATER

It used to be I could turn in my chair
because moments came up like trains
and passed as easily as fields
passed me sitting on a train.
But no longer. My inner ear hums.
Things go a little off, like water standing
where water shouldn't be.
I put my hand down here,
and here is over there.
Crossing a room, I stop by a table
and can't stop. Sometimes
when I stop by a table,
I am not there yet.
Now and then, the boards on the floor
tip a little and I tip a little and, angling,
have to brace myself for the wall.
I go along it with my hands.
It's like they are walking along the wall.
Windows I don't enjoy much.
I look out but my mind won't go out.
Windows make me look back at myself.

I MIGHT BREAK, I MIGHT DISAPPEAR

I am standing in the doorway in my snowsuit.
I love my snowsuit, I want to wear it all the time.
I am so excited that I see someone,
probably myself, across the field,
emerging from the falling snow.
I don't move for fear the person won't come,
or will come and will leave me. I know,
I am just standing there, but I am afraid
I might break, I might disappear,
or not be able to speak when I speak.
It's the snow. It piles
and piles, yet nothing falls over.
The first time I saw snow
I was looking up and up
at white coming down everywhere,
and mother looking down at me
was saying snow.
She meant white landing on my face
and hands was snow. Snow she said again
and caught it on her tongue. She meant taste too!
I caught snow on my tongue. I even said it.
And best of all, I heard myself say snow, snow.

SLIP AWAY

I'm getting ready for people coming over,
something I am not very good at,
but I suppose that is an excuse.
When you're old, it takes so much time to fool yourself.
So I should tidy up, I guess,
but there aren't enough chairs.
I don't need one, I'll be greeting people. Soon
people are talking and smiling so hard
their dentures show.
That's my cue. I will slip away,
float off, high above the house,
and look down on everyone.
To them, I am still here.
Someone may wonder and ask
if anyone has seen me in a while.
people will say, Oh she's around,
you can count on her; or a child shout,
She's hiding! Other children squeal
and the grownups play a game for the children
of looking for me. All around the house they look
and call out through the children yelling
and running after them. When the kids get tired
maybe the grownups can't decide what to do about me,
not right then anyway.
I'd like that. It would help keep me going.

MEN AND FAT

Men and fat, you get past them both
when you are old, but I'd take a diet
to worry about over all these pills.
I can see it now; I give up the ghost
with my arm raised to my wide open mouth
and a huge pink pill in the palm of my hand.

Eskimos, about to die, just walk off,
right? saving their families all sorts
of trouble. I wouldn't mind. There aren't
any ice floes around here, but we have
something just as deadly: parking lots.
I can get run over there. Probably though,

I'd get bumped and sued and the police
would haul me back to my family,
who would put the clampers on me or, worse,
entertain me. Better to be locked up with
a snowy TV and that old hound Caboose. He's
got one eye and the mange. He makes sense.

BAD DAY

Don't assume I am writing anything down,
or plan to, or that I can stand reading it,
even when there is nothing to do, or that
I have any idea of what I am going to write;
and don't think for a minute it's any fun.
It's not. These are dumb notions I won't
explain, except they run around like cats
and writing is the only way to trap them, rid
them. It beats biting my lips to bits. Crazy?
There is not enough left of me to go crazy.
People old as me don't go crazy. We dribble
away, a part at a time, and the live parts,
they are too dumb to know what else to do,
even when the part next to them breaks.
Don't come after these papers either. They
go with me, stuffed into my clothes, see.
When the clothes shrivel and blow open,
the papers float into the nothing they talk to.

GLINT

You see the chair out there in the field?
I love it. And the two big stones?
They are so smooth they could have
rolled in the ocean for years. This was once
an ocean floor. I like to imagine that.
The two big stones, I call them sun stones.
They send sunlight out and out across the valley.
I imagine my words going out there too,
when I speak. So I think hard
about what I am going to say. The stream passing
in front of me, I watch it and pretend
the words form in the stream.
The stream helps me think.
The stream helps me not to think, too. To get here,
the stream comes miles across the valley,
down from the mountains, snowcapped year round,
mountains you see only now and then
as if, through the night, they pull away again.
I would like to move like the mountains
and move like the stream, too.
Even in a mist, the stream has a glint to it.

BLUE BLUE HAIR

I am on the floor, on my back. I must have fallen,
knocked myself cuckoo. Oblong, everything
is oblong. My mouth tastes bad. Some of it I think
got turned inside out when I fell. The rug
smells of ammonia. I hum my slow song about almonds
to soothe me. Down here, I can lick my own blood.
As a kid, I could wrap a hose around a tree,
then turn the water on hard, make that hose
jump like a snake. Not any more.
If only I could hear a good banjo,
I'd lie here until I was cold liver.
As long as the bridge group of mine
doesn't find out. They would like nothing better
than to get something on me and razz me
until I break out. Sure, I put silverware
in their coat pockets and try to be there
when they pull it out. You can see the idea
cross their faces, slow as a bug,
as if that blue blue hair dulls the brain.

I WON'T NEED LEGS THERE

I weigh less than some dogs,
and where I am going I want to be smaller still,
especially my head, thick and sagging.
I won't need legs there.
My hands, poor things,
more and more like bird wings.
I hide them. I have started to go—
when I turn in my chair and wave to someone leaving,
the person isn't leaving, I am.
I think of waving
but the air doesn't work
and I'm smaller, lighter, and passing through.

DO NOT LET THEM TAKE ME AWAY IF NAKED

Do not let them take me away if naked
they find me out on the lawn with the Purple Martins
swooping around their birdhouses
and me pretending the Purple Martins listen
when I speak. I say that to pass the time;
I don't know when I will die.
Besides, the night grass is wet and cold.

Do not let them take me away if naked
they find me down on the dock,
or leaning against a piling and facing out
over the water, or in a rowboat tied to the dock,
on the floorboards, leaning back
with my head on the seat in the stern
and getting dizzy from the stars.

Do not let them take me away if naked
they find me cast off from the dock, floating
around the pond, under what we have for clouds
and a moon. I am ninety-six. Who is to say
I won't know when my time comes;
and I don't want any clothes getting in the way.
That would be like leaving in a sack.

SHOVELING SNOW WHILE IT IS STILL SNOWING

When you are down to your slow mind and fingers,
it is hard to push and push to clear your mind
for new thoughts. I try. Today, when I finally
got out there in the open of my mind,
back came shoveling snow during a snowfall.
It felt good, although I was getting nowhere.
In a big snow, you just keep shoveling.
It's a knack to shovel while it's snowing,
a kind of concentration that cannot depend on results.
So how you think about something is important.
Think how many creatures die by being eaten.
Some are alive even while being eaten.
Some people see their death walk up to them.
Creatures that die in one season and return
in another, perhaps they are the lucky ones.
They are certainly the pretty ones. Imagine
dying beautiful. That is the best reason
for having people around you when you die.
Maybe not. I may have this altogether wrong.

FULL HEAT THAT FLUTTERS

I spread the fingers on my hand and stare through the spaces.
I like time with little in it,
like a puddle, something but with little in it.
I am getting smaller, and I'm trying to keep growing too,
in here, in my heart. This means I must make room
in my heart. Must move people on, years and years of people.
Friends grow roots thick as rope.
Friends cling, they die and don't let go.
Ivy on the woodpile and the trunks of trees, I cut it
but it won't come off.
It's like my friends. I have to rip it off.
I tell friends I love them but I don't want to see them
all the time. They pout
like their cats. And worse, they let their worries
squeeze them into twigs.
I call these "the frights." They're like boils:
rub them and they get worse.
I don't want to go in my sleep.
I like the porch. I'll pull my chair along to hold the shade.
I want light, high morning light, and a breeze.
And heat, full heat that flutters.

HOW THEY'RE DANCING IS HOW THEY EAT

Boats come in over fields. They nose
down and up where the wind scooped the fields
and left high grass flat on its side.
If the sky boats are coming for me, they are too big,

and I want one more bright hot day
I can walk out of, onto the broad lawn shadows
of an oak, and look up into high branches.
Wind way up there and cool grass under my feet!

My lungs fill. My breathing drops near sleep.
I eavesdrop on birds. I love eels,
how they dig one end into the bottom and sway,
like sea grass, just like sea grass
for passersby; how they're dancing is how they eat.

II
NIGHT FISHING

◆

◆

I know what I know,
I know what I said.
We come and we go:
That's a thing that I keep
At the back of my head.

—PAUL SIMON, "DIAMONDS ON THE SOLES OF HER SHOES"

THE ONE POLAR BEAR

You know how in the zoo most of the polar bears
look good—big, white, eating, and lying around—
and when a polar bear stands up, wow! And there's
one polar bear by itself. Look closely, you can
see its coat worn in spots to the bone, sores
the size of plates. The bear lumbers to the bars
and rubs, right on the sores. Sure they get worse!
And you can see the sores getting worse, redder
bigger. The attendants, can they do anything
about it? Ask them. Nothing works. Nothing
makes the bear happy. You know why? The bear
doesn't want to be happy. Maybe the bear
doesn't even want to be a bear, be anything.
I know about rubbing yourself away on the bars.

DOWN A WELL

When you first floated a hello
to my hello, you lifted the lid
of my skin and came in. Now,
when you leave, I'm inside out.
I drive to find a place to drive.
The road hisses to the rain,
curls its toes. It knows the park
will pull me over unless,
right now, I kiss you again here
and there and here and lose
my hands in your rolling hair.

THE FOX

It's not how sharp your teeth are
or how quickly you strike
and snap the chick's neck,

but that wind and wet and dark
are always there before you in the grass
and your scent, it drifts this

way and that. There a meadow
you must cross and the moon is
full. You are there. You are

not there. Nothing but a shadow
or two. Wait, what was that?
Was it like this a moment ago?

It's hard to tell, what with the wind
in the grass, and the moonlight.
Then no wind. And clouds, slow

and lit on the side toward
the moon. It's hard
to tell. Even now.

WAX STUNS PRECISION GRINDING, SWEEPS TO CITY SOFTBALL TITLE

I missed our B-League streak,
the playoffs, upsetting the A-League champs,
the last play, last out, a pop-up you squeezed
into that old glove of yours, then the roll
of whoops and beer flapping the trophy bowl.
And everyone toasted that night you called
saying come back from wherever, you didn't care,
just get there, pound the bar door
locked to keep everyone looped from leaving.

And next season, be there, you said, commit;
I'm there, shaking out the bat bag,
that bat clunking sound, sweet as the first
time you slide your fingers into your glove
and work the creased pocket with your fist.
Spring practice. I see it. Rake the infield against
bad hops. Grip each bat. Step in, back foot
deep in the box. Take your 20 cuts. Just
get good wood on the ball. Spray line shots
to every field. Roll a few to the fence
and, head down, run the last one out.

Now it's your turn to shag flies in light rain.
You peddle in, peddle out, get an angle,
lock the ball into your glove and squeeze.
Then lob the throw in to save your arm.

Crack! A hit that sounds like a rifle shot,
that you don't spot coming off the bat; it lifts,
accelerating, and clears you by a couple of feet.
With a good jump you might have picked it
from the air, over your shoulder, on the run,
the ball nesting in the webbing of your glove.

Few games endure the rain. A couple of innings
and the ump works up a scowl to call it off.
Then you tromp on down to the tavern
for the talk about how this season
we'll hit the cutoff man and move
our runners along. Not like last year,
how many runners did we leave at third?
A long fly would have brought them in.
Maybe that ties it up or gives us the win.
Yeah, make that a burger and a beer
and a round here for my friends.
This year we'll go all the way
if we swing the bat, play good ball.

HALLOWEEN OF THE SUDDEN HAND

We wait for dark, then, dressed commando,
move as one, like cilia. We work backyards and sheds,
hanging heads we made from junk and painted loony
in my cellar. Once little kids scarf the candy
and front porch lights go off, we stalk
the shadow side of the pointed-turret house
where old crazy lady lives with her retarded son.
We creep our pole up to a lit window on the second floor
and tap our brown-paper head with green marbles for eyes.
No luck. Gently we lift it over to the next window,
a dark window. A hand comes out,
pats our head and takes out one eye. After that,
anyone messing with the old lady answers to us.

SNAKE MOUTH

My trap was wire, double coiled, with good line
and a new Navy knot. I called it Snake Mouth
and lay in bed, springing it in the dark,
out over rocks into low wood where the creek
turned brown, almost black, and pooled deep.
I swung the trap out, swat, in the middle,
put a rock on the end of the line, with a little
slack, and sat cross-legged on the moss.

Shadows ran the water. Rain beat the water.
The line sprang tight, shot over the bank.
A bank tree lurched, a big branch split
off at the trunk white as chicken meat.
The creek bulged, started to lift.
Birds racketed all the way home.

COMING HOME

Sometimes I need to be there for a while
before I can really be there, as if I need to
sneak up on returning home to you
—say, park down street and, coming up to the house,

set my hand in the mailbox,
say, palm down, to see if I left
a message, and think what
the message might be, between the mailbox and the house;

draw my fingers along the ridges of the mailbox,
and think about messages
sliding along the ridges,
sliding in and out under the ceiling,

the nicely arched ceiling of the mailbox,
and, before leaving, lift the flap that hangs, when
open, like a tongue;
lift the mailbox flap gently enough

not to disturb the space
you like me to reach for you through,
that you enjoy your own sifting through
—a space you float to allow us both

our own leaning in and leaning out,
a kind of transparent balloon
we can move toward one
another within. I'm already

at the front door, feeling the key
find the keyhole; and quickly
I'm between the door opening
and hearing you coming toward me,

between your continuing to appear
more clearly and your arms opening. I slip
my arms under your arms, lift
you and, for a long deep breath, hold you aloft.

THE MAN WHO CAN'T WAIT
FOR BURGLARS

Yes yes yes, to make sure no one breaks into my house
I double check all doors and windows and have a dazzle
of a plan set and, by my bed, my light, Big Blinder,
and my electric net when he gets in downstairs somehow.
I'm on the landing, behind the clock, with Big Blinder.
He glints and bounds for the cellar. I step out:
mistake. He lifts me by the ankles, raps my head
on the piano, and heads for the control panel. Flick,
parrots screech through the ventilation. Flick,
the furnace blubbers, and bats, crazed, zing and zang.
I jam his pocket override beeper gewgaw,
and reverse it back at him. He lights up like Jell-O,
yells, retreats to the bathroom, and slams the door.
I release laughing gas through the bathtub faucet.
I hum and imagine him playing the game
Kiss-the-mirror-kiss-your-nose. I tiptoe
to the bathroom, step in, and demo his would-be
dismemberment. Oh, I hope he comes back soon!

ODYSSEUS TURNS PRO

He drove the ball to the base of a large tree
and as he came striding down the fairway,
his fans, men and women alike, sensed
he was summoning his forces. That's

how they put it: summoning his forces.
Even with his seemingly impossible lie,
he seemed relaxed, walking back out onto
the fairway to eye the green. He looked

so clear about what he was going to do
that his fans thought they knew too and
just couldn't find the words. Back he
cranked his club in that slight crouch of his.

For all his fans could tell he was about to
drive the ball into the tree. No wonder then
that the shot that exploded from the tree and rose
to the trap-rimmed green became legend.

WHEN THE DIRT WON'T STAY DOWN

I come through the door with my ancestors
on either side of me. I don't see them. I'm not
supposed to. Their accompanying me means
I connect back through time. Some people don't.
They are lost. I'm not supposed to worry
about them. My ancestors intend to make me selfish
before I die. They needle me. I'm sitting patiently
behind someone at a red light, and they make me
lean on the horn. I'm dozing when suddenly
I feel I had better not move quickly or I'll break.
They love doing this and are quick to say
they are only doing their job of showing me
that I connect back through time. Yet I'm home
only a few days when friends look at me funny,
"When you're around, the dirt won't stay down."
What's that supposed to mean? That I'm some
sort of weirdy? That I lift the dead for kicks?
Maybe I should put a sign in front of my house:
the home of Flying Snake Brain.

WHEN THE BIG BLUE LIGHT COMES
A WHIRLING UP BEHIND

Leaning back in the white vinyl of your rear-high
Mustang, forest green gleaming in as big a Saturday sun
as any June day could make, perfect for letting her out,
when the big blue light comes a whirling up behind
and pulls you over. The trooper fills your window.
Hey kid, let's see your license if you have one.
You fumble it out, and the registration
from the tight glove compartment. He lumbers back
to his car, sits under the whirling light while traffic
goes by like planes. How much is there to write?
Here he comes. He hands you your license and ticket.
Drive like that again, kid, and you'll never drive again.
In your rearview mirror, he walks back to his car
and cruises out into traffic. You wait, you wait longer.
Then start up, look, signal, pull out and stick
in the right lane. Your speedometer won't stay steady.
You try to breathe all the way through yourself. You'd
like to tell him where he can go shine his leather.
You'd like a button on your dash that says WINGS.

A MAN ON A BICYCLE

If I squint just right into the sun
and the handlebars don't jiggle,
I see double stacks of hay bales
as ziggurats. They hold the field
like temples, and Queen Anne's Lace
lines the roadside ditches.
Around ten at night, quail sound
their mating call, which gives me
the willies, like when a peacock
stared into the side mirror
of a pickup truck, dangling upside down,
the mirror that is. In lovemaking,
there is the nimble, twang, and vichyssoise
and how your bones become bamboo
in the slow scattering of feathers around them.

TRAFFIC JAM ON THE
ROSS ISLAND BRIDGE

for Dennis Meiners

I am knuckled in here on the Ross Island Bridge,
heading west, toward the West Hills of Portland.
The hills are ridged by trees in silhouette
against the sunset. Strands of clouds loll over the trees,
sink into them, and snag. One strand settles in the trees
like a big, gray nest. If there is no Northwest bird
that lays its eggs in such a nest, inventing it is my job.
My potter friend and I will envision the bird.
I will tell my friend that white sunset
comes down on the nest and shimmers it;
and darkness, thick with rain, pushes the light
down into the trees. There is not enough sky for rain
to get down easily. The rain is slowed by rain
below it. Why hurry? This is Oregon, rain is lazy here.
Wind shoots rain up in sheets that topple back
and fall through themselves. Between the tree line and
the darkness falling are planes of light,
measuring miles across. Rain does not faze them.
These slabs slide through themselves,
across the entire city. I'd love to have one hover
over my backyard some early evening,
and take friends out to toast it.

THE ONE TIME I GOT BACK TO MY BIRTH

I tried many times: I scattered tasty food scraps
across the ground and imagined some sort of animal
getting there first. This worked up my saliva,
which helped me lay hold of my inside fat.
Still, the food scraps, by the time I found them again,
were pretty bad, all caked with mud, and stinking.
I straddled the food scrap, ate, vomited sometimes,
and moved on. It was easy to pass out,
and then that was that. Just a big headache
to show for trying to get back to my birth.
But if I could keep going, from one scrap to the next,
I could draw my fat out and get going pretty fast.
I had to finish, though, before the crossover
to my birth or I would splatter all over the place,
and then it would be weeks of blackouts
and nightmares and chills. I always saw this coming,
so I always chickened out of trying
to get back to my birth, except this one time.
I didn't have time to worry about it I guess,
I just shot back. I must have hit it just right.
That's my story, that's how it happened for me.

AFTER TEDIOUS ARGUING

Come on back and let it go.
Vent until the shutters clatter,
until you feel like jazz, like
a palace cat named Viscous,
like a cello on a blue chaise lounge
—yes, vent until you feel much
too good, much too sleek
and sassy, to bother to
razz me, so relaxed
you're a motel
with its back to the ocean;
You're a Lincoln Continental,
polished, parked, with tinted glass.
Passersby pucker up and sigh.
Here, these arms of mine,
fuzzed dangles
of mildew and cardboard,
take them, make them
swing to stay around. And this
used and confused flesh
with its shrill jury of nerves,
flap it like a scatter rug.

NIGHT FISHING

The water is a glaze like loneliness at ease
with itself. I cast and close my eyes for the whir
out across the water, the line striking the surface
and sinking. I like waiting for it to settle on the bottom,
then jig it up a little. I imagine the lure in the utter dark.
I play it lightly. Fish rise. Just shy of the surface,
they play their glints off the moon on the water.
I see too my own loneliness. It's not too big
and it breathes easily. Soon, it may pretend it's rain.
Rain blurs the water. There is nothing wrong
with rain. I take a deep breath and cast and cast.

SOME OF THE DEAD GO TO THE CITY

Some of the dead go to the city. They can hide there,
they don't have to talk. They can't. They love
to sit out on front porches. All the cars and busses
and neon signs and people on the sidewalk
and people crossing the street
and yelling. City people talk to themselves a lot,
talk to all the people they are at once.
The dead love this. They nod and shuffle their hands.
The dead have trouble, though, keeping their heads up
and their mouths from sagging open,
so they lean their heads against a wall,
and hold their mouths closed. Attention they don't like,
especially from little kids who point and talk loud.
Even in summer, the dead wear overcoats, like drunks.
They can stare you down, scare you away,
but you might tell someone, and they don't move fast.
They hate trying, they hate to do much of anything
but sitting on a front porch when it's not too hot,
traffic is snarled and radios are blaring.

III

MALENESS AND VIOLENCE

◆

◆

Not me. Not that. But not nothing, either. A "something" that I do not recognize as a thing.
A weight of meaninglessness about which there is nothing insignificant, crushes me.

—JULIA KRISTEVA, *POWERS OF HORROR*

THE BRINK

This chair and window and day, dear things
crowding me crazy—me, Mr. hi ho here
and ho hum blow your nose over there. I don't care,
anything to keep the old memory rash from heating up.
I can't help fiddling with it. I sweat. I guess
I scratch some scabs off and dizzy out,
woozy as a weed. When I land a reason to go out,
the reason caves in at the door as if it were kidding.
I lie back down and listen to the rain plink plonk
the broken gutter puddle. I make the sound, too.
With each drip, I pop my lips. And do some humming.
I should take the garbage out, I know that.
My chest has a drummer in it who is a showoff.
I can settle if I don't look at the phone.
Wads of phlegm break up on their own.
I pretend I am on a long train that sleeps by day.
At night I float, tiny, from one page of a comic book
to the next. I put words in the ovals.
A good little thriller can come out of this.
Time for sit-ups. Look at those toes, the little rabbits!
I am a moving van, empty, doors ajar, with a stack
of tarps in the corner behind the driver.
Here is the plan: I will take one room of the house
at a time and quietly. When the racket comes,
I never cook. Never make salads. No knives.
I sit on my hands. The racket comes at night, too,
when I'm asleep; I'm yelling before I know
what I am saying. The same racket I try to
wash out when I shower over and over again,
that I eat out when I eat and don't eat.

THE CLEARING

Where darkness made a cave
with passageways, like a body,
I hid my gentleness as a boy
and yelled and sang my own language.
They said they loved me,
the ugly little animals,
even when I stepped on them.
Then the clearing. I stared for hours
at the clearing. If I could get to the center
standing, I wouldn't be afraid all the time.
I start across. So does someone
across from me, walking
toward me at the same rate,
someone who looks much like me,
except his hair is combed
and he has a dumb smile.
He could kill me, he wouldn't mind,
and it would be my fault.

WHAT SCARED ME AS A BOY
WAS NOT MY SEX

What scared me as a boy was not my sex,
my father, or the world, but how calmly
I joined others in taking a creature apart,
like a cat over its stunned prey,

looking away, smacking it from time to time,
and the thick quiet, the prolonging,
the same quiet as in my dream
of staring out across the huge fish I stand on,

shoving my hands into air holes
on the fish's back and making spouts.
I bring a desk chair up on its back,
stick in an umbrella and, at night,

make little fires. The fish doesn't cry out,
doesn't even move. I think it wants me there,
down through its dying. Or is it giving birth
and taking care of the child will be my job?

VICTIM

He came at her, enraged. She froze,
just as she had the last time.
In the hospital, when she was again conscious,
he slobbered promises until she forgave him.
She dreamed of fish,
little fish that chanced by her sea cave
and she closed her eyes as she closed her jaws
over them. She didn't leave her cave
for fear her swimming would drive light
through her body and creatures would mock
and nibble her until she was helpless.

As he came at her, enraged, again, she felt herself
shrinking. She became too small to finish
the laundry, too small to get the children
off to school. She needed time to think
before he beat her. She stepped aside.
He stumbled past her, fell,
and came at her again.
She was thinking of wet laundry
and the children, who had already missed
so much school. She jumped aside.
He thrashed past her, turned, and charged.
She brought her knee up into his groin
and scratched his face. He went over.
She fell on him, bit him,
buried her mouth in his neck
until people, yelling, pulled her off.

From time to time now,
she turns her hands over and over,
looking, she says, for things that crawl
from under her blouse onto her wrists.

OIL SPILL

The ocean is leather in slow motion.
Waves don't break, they squat and slide.
Stick a finger in—thick as fudge
up and down the beach;

and the fixed, brown bubbles
mean death by suffocation.
May the men who did this
boil and roll in a seal coat of oil;

and may their superiors
join us and our neighbors
on our knees
to scrub this beach to the bone.

If they are unwilling,
may they stand naked facing a mirror
and hear behind them, forever,
the fawning and sniveling of underlings.

INMATES WORK AT THE CHICKEN FACTORY

From your asylum to the chicken-bone bin
and back you bear a silence that seeps
rough couples dozing on the town green.
Children look. Parents mumble as if asleep

and roll away from your brittle walk,
your gaze, your inmate clothes
that make me look for others
watching. No adults look. What does

it take to choke down chicken bones
grinding to pulp and smoke that stinks
and drips from crusted stacks?
I've followed you to the asylum cyclone

fence and wondered what your lungs,
your heart, take in. The town acts dumb.
So you squint, you dawdle,
you walk through numb,

pretending if you look up you stumble.
The town is a place you
drag your stench back through.

DUMBO DINER

When the chemical waste plant went up,
we didn't ask ourselves, could it kill us?
—except me, here, at Dumbo Diner,
the place with the elephant ears on top.

A couple of years later, after bingo,
folks got to talking about how hard
it had become to sell a home; it was time
to run the plant out of town. Next morning,
folks were knocking on doors. The old guy
next door, never spoken to me, over he comes
and tells me to get on downtown
to the gun shop and hardware store.

We loaded up, tromped out to the plant
and burned it down. Now the town looks like
it's been fertilized. Maybe gray toxic weeds will sprout,
grow huge, fight it out with helicopters. In a few days,
the first scavengers. They might get the toxic tick.
I hope their blood bleaches like the city stream.
If they come downtown, I've got souvenirs,
nice toxic waste packets, sandwich bags
filled that I loop onto their cars.

If they don't leave town, I'll help them along.
The window here facing down street, I kicked it out.
I don't like flying glass when I roll a few rounds
over their heads. I've got this automatic
bolted on the counter. I like the action. I like
the swivel of this counter stool. The minute
the fed flunkies step out of their cars, the sidewalk
at their feet will whistle. They want more, I'll oblige.
They want an investigation, I'm an investigation.
I'm here at Dumbo Diner. Look for the ears.

ASH

We're afraid of sun and hope for rain.
A clear day means the ash will blow.
We wear our masks or stay inside.

The ash is in our clothes, our teeth, grains
of ash that float like snow.
We attune to plumes, shifts of wind,

And sandbags by the sewer drains.
We're told to keep the driving slow.
It's breathing, though, that gets us down;

And if particles sift through anything,
so the tourist trade may be a record low,
so what? What of the nuclear plant up the road?

All we hear is the old refrain:
temporarily closed. Yet the volcano,
45 miles from downtown Portland,

May blow again.
A lava dome begins to grow
We walk our daughter to a nearby pond

To feed the ducks.——Here they come,
look how the little ducks have grown!
We see their crowns

Covered with ash, their beaks, wings.
Why don't they go?
—Shoo, shoo! Get out of town!

We should go back now,
stay inside, check the TV and radio.
Rain just means the ash won't blow.

THE MAN WHO LIVES ON AIR

Last week the town left. A sofa squats
at the bus stop and takes the snow.
When the plant closed completely down,
families swore they would never leave.
That was talk. A few months of scissors
wind, first out of one direction and then
the opposite, had houses whistling. Next
you couldn't get buried here. If only
the interstate hadn't veered south and left
a truckstop by a silo. Then the tornado.
The houses fight for their lives. I know
the screech of a roof lifting, nails cringing
and, whoosh, the roof's gone, the shack
is sheered in half. I'll take a dull wind
shuffling down Main Street, clanking signs,
rumbling houses left to sink and heave
in thaws. Some days, I hammer planks until
it feels I'm hammering every building here.
When a house cracks, I prop it. If it goes,
I raze it, I swear, and lay down the dust.

JUNK IS MY LIFE

Junk is my life, like the sign says, and I am dying.
The stuff people bring in nowadays, they lug it up
to the counter as if they are doing me a favor.
No thanks, I say. Sometimes they go nuts and
we get a hot one going. Take it out, I suggest,
to the parking lot, back over it a couple of times,

Give it a little original shape. This one guy, he got
so hot he did just that, flattened it, screeching
back and forth. Wish I had him on the old P.A.
Dropped his rear axle in a rut I left for guys like
him. Takes me to court. Loses. Later, the judge
suggests I add something to my sign about how I

Don't take any old thing. Sure, why not? Maybe
the judge will come by to check. I bet he has some
good junk. I'll have to wangle. Have to chat
standards, yeah, whatever happened to standards?
Get him boasting about what he still owns. Get him
back in the store. Like I said, junk is my life.

BIG SHOT GRACES THE OLD BAR & GRILL

What you say? What you crazy?
It's me, I'm back! Hey, ugly,
here's looking at you. You guys,
the old gang. Barflies. Barflies.

Maybe I buy this place as a tax deduction,
list you deadbeats as a bunch of luncheons.
Ha! Not bad, huh? Shake. If you want
to smile, get some teeth. Doesn't

anyone do anything here? Lifts the blinds!
When a guy comes home, it's a high time
he's deserving. If anyone got out of here,
remember what we promised? Sure,

we wrote in blood: we'd throw a party
for him. You just didn't figure on me,
right? No, not the little fat kid
you beat up all the time. You did,

admit it. Now's your chance.
Hey, don't all talk at once.
That's a joke. I'm kidding.
O.K., I'm not kidding.

You're an old debt
I've come to collect
on. Probably you
haven't a clue

what I'm saying.
So listen, I'm paying.
Drinks are on me.
This party for you is for me.

THE DISTANCE

You lean down close enough to blow me over
and say, "Don't need anything you can't
buy, take or, with your own hands, make.
Do that and you'll be like me. That's
what you want. You want to be my son."

And when you left, you left your distance
for me to feed on. Stuff came up. "Spit
it out, boy; so people deserve our trust,
huh? Grow up, assume the worst."

I didn't know your tough-guy talk was smoke
to cover up your dry martini heart. You took
your disappointment out on me, a kid,
and my kid brother. That's gutless.
I'd love to crack your distance now across

your grave. Just what you'd like: I'd prove
you right, I'd never get away. So here, I give
you back your distance, all I've dislodged,
year by year, chunk by rancid
chunk. A little boy can take a lot.

PULLING IT OUT

From here, in the center of the field, I can see
all around and I am sure no one is watching,
I lift my hands to my mouth, cupped, as if
to call out, open my mouth wide, reach in
and pull on the slippery thing. A better grip,
a harder pull, and it moves, way down
in my stomach. I squeeze, my chest loosens.
Some of it comes up into my mouth.
Then the end flops out and dangles. I lean
over, yank on it. Up it comes. I drop it.
It wriggles on the ground, stinks, bounces.
I want to jump up and down on it, squish it.
It's blind, I think, oozing and rolling over. Maybe
it just wanted a place to rest or a place to live.
Then again, if I hadn't done anything, probably
it would have eaten me out from the inside.

INFORMATION BLACKOUT

What the government called an information blackout
is what it did to the people's tongues,
and when the people planted the tongues,
hut radios jumped the word out, over the border,
the radio operator dragged out, deafened,
his hands smashed to the consistency of cornmeal.

When the world appealed, the government announced
a new machine for agricultural reform. Boys
chasing after it saw the pincer contraption
on top of the tank crank into a sapling,
close, and pop the sapling from the earth.
The boys knew before they knew,
their mouths sliding from their faces.

People mourned the sapling and buried it.
The government made one of the people
the Death-Counter. He counted,
but only birds, and the people
sang of their dead rising above the birds.
Fear, the Ever-Long Snake, could not find a home,
for no 12 houses in a row fell silent at once.

Strong people, with the shine of hard rock
in their eyes, who could look at soldiers
and see nothing, they were gathered
to go into the desert, to work the roads.
Marching out of town, they had to sing as
they passed the television truck and reviewing stand.

Troops sent out to check on the work crews
did not return, and a renowned fanatic,
flying his choice plane loaded with poison spray,
returned without the planned fanfare,
muttering of birds blackening his cockpit.

The government spiked deserters above town wells,
their wounds dripping into the well water.
The townspeople cut them down, and, at night,
sneaked them into the barracks and stretched them out,
dead, on empty cots, under blankets, in the dark.

Foot soldiers, made to go into the desert,
straggled back, admitting they had not gotten far.
Their dogs had deserted them early,
and the stars became too bright to sleep.
The solders spoke of a whir out across the desert
like many birds gathering for flight.

THEY CAME HERE TO DIE

They came here to die, the elegant young men
at the cafe across the street
in the full sun of this Sunday afternoon in San Francisco.
A row of tables lines the sidewalk,
and behind them, against the wall, the young men
have placed all the chairs, facing out.
They lean back in the chairs against the building
and gaze across the street,
across the square behind me,
for all I know across their whole journey here
to this day, to this cafe in San Francisco.
They don't talk. They don't look at me either.
Probably, they pretty much despise me for staring at them,
or they don't care.
I suppose, if I learned I was dying,
I would leave people I knew
to be with people who understand.
I could join my dying to their dying.
Nobody could tell me to disappear.

MORICHES BAY

I didn't know what my brother meant
when he said the sound of the explosion
reached Quogue and he still didn't know
what had exploded when he and other volunteers
gathered uptown, before dawn, and drove west
to Center Moriches, to the bay where wreckage
of a huge plane lay out across the night-gray water.
My brother told me volunteers extended the line
out into the bay, that they waded in gingerly.
What was passed to each man, each man
passed on: a piece of fuselage, a piece of corpse,
a lobster pot long on the bottom. He said
this got harder, all the volunteers said so.
The people's souls had not moved on;
the volunteers could feel their souls
coming through. They could hardly look
at what their hands received. So from time
to time, they looked across the bay,
across the inlet, to the ocean. It was brightening
over the ocean where the sun would soon
come up. There wasn't yet room
for the souls of the dead to rise off the bay.